GLOEM GOSPEL HYMNAL

WITH 50 PROMISES OF GOD AVAILABLE TO ALL BELIEVERS

Unless otherwise indicated, all Scripture quotations are taken from the New King James Version of the Bible.

GLOEM GOSPEL HYMNAL

ISBN: 978-1-989969-43-4

Copyright © 2022 by Global Emancipation Ministries – Calgary

Published by

GLOEM Publishing House

Calgary, AB, Canada

Email: info@gloem.org; Website: www.gloem.org

Printed in Canada. All rights reserved.

No part of this book may be reproduced or transmitted in any form or by any means, electronic or mechanical, including photocopying, recording, or by any information storage and retrieval system, without permission in writing from the publisher, except for evangelical and/or spiritual education purposes only.

PREFACE

GLOEM Gospel Hymnal is a collection of special hymns compiled for the purpose of connecting our hearts with God's Heart in worship. The Almighty God desires that His children worship Him in spirit and in truth (John 4:23-24).

In addition to these spiritual songs, some promises of God that are available to all His children are included for our confident engagement.

Hebrews 6:13-17 (NKJV) says:
"For when God made a promise to Abraham, because He could swear by no one greater, He swore by Himself, saying 'Surely blessing I will bless you, and multiplying I will multiply you'. And so, after he had patiently endured, he obtained the promise. For men indeed swear by the greater, and an oath for confirmation is for them an end of all dispute. Thus God, determining to show more abundantly to the heirs of promise the immutability of His counsel, confirmed it by an oath, that by two immutable things, in which it is impossible for God to lie, we might have strong consolation, who have fled for refuge to lay hold of the hope set before us."

When a promise is made, one may be doubtful as to whether the fellow making the promise will fulfill it or not; but when the fellow backs up the promise with an oath – swearing by someone greater than himself, every form of doubt will disappear because the fellow is now bound to fulfill what he has promised. This was the case with God and Abraham. He gave him a promise, and since there is no one greater than Him, He decided to swear by Himself. He put His Almightiness, Holiness, Righteousness, Most Highness and Sovereignty on the line; and sure enough, He fulfilled what He promised him – He blessed him and greatly multiplied him.

The text says God is determined to show to us too being the heirs of the promise He made to our father Abraham the immutability of His counsel so that we can be rest assured that what He has promised us, He will surely fulfill if only we will exhibit faith and patience as our father did – verses 15-17.

The word 'immutability' according to Oxford Advanced Learner's Dictionary means something that cannot be changed, something that will never change. That's what God is trying to get across. Since He will never tell a lie (Numbers 23:19), He is saying He will fulfill all He has promised us, without changing any of them. This is because He had sworn by Himself to do so.

This Hymn Book in your hands is a collection of 61 songs carefully selected to worship, praise and minister unto God for His Person, integrity and commitment to fulfilling His Words in our lives.

The 50 promises of God it also contains are available to all believers who dare to claim them. As you sing unto Him and claim these promises, you will experience their manifestations in your own life and your joy shall overflow in Jesus' Name.

Anthony Adefarakan

President, GLOEM Canada.

HYMN NUMBERS AND OPENING LINES

Hymn 01 – Faithfulness does not depend…

Hymn 02 – My God answers prayers…

Hymn 03 – I will praise Thee, King of glory…

Hymn 04 – Holy Father, so gracious and faithful…

Hymn 05 – Adonai be Thou magnified…

Hymn 06 – This is my season of favour…

Hymn 07 – All hail the pow'r of Jesus' name…

Hymn 08 – Praise to the Lord, the Almighty…

Hymn 09 – Praise, my soul, the King of heaven…

Hymn 10 – O for a thousand tongues to sing…

Hymn 11 – O worship the King all-glorious above…

Hymn 12 – Praise Him! praise Him! Jesus, our blessed Redeemer…

Hymn 13 – To God be the glory, great things He hath done…

Hymn 14 – O God, our help in ages past…

Hymn 15 – Great is Thy faithfulness…

Hymn 16 – I am so glad that our Father in heaven…

Hymn 17 – How sweet the name of Jesus sounds…

Hymn 18 – How sweet the name of Jesus sounds in a believer's ear…

Hymn 19 – Crown Him with many crowns…

Hymn 20 – There's not a Friend like the lowly Jesus…

Hymn 21 – Breathe on me, Breath of God…

Hymn 22 – There shall be showers of blessing…

Hymn 23 – The great Physician now is near…

Hymn 24 – Thy kingdom come, O God…

Hymn 25 – Have you been to Jesus for the cleansing pow'r…

Hymn 26 – Lord, I hear of show'rs of blessing…

Hymn 27 – Rock of Ages, cleft for me…

Hymn 28 – Jesus only is our message.

Hymn 29 – Would you be free from your burden of sin…

Hymn 30 – We have heard the joyful sound…

Hymn 31 – I'm pressing on the upward way…

Hymn 32 – Blessed assurance, Jesus is mine…

Hymn 33 – I need Thee ev'ry hour…

Hymn 34 – When peace like a river attendeth my way…

Hymn 35 – Onward, Christian soldiers…

Hymn 36 – Stand up, stand up for Jesus…

Hymn 37 – Christian, seek not yet repose…

Hymn 38 – My Jesus, I love Thee…

Hymn 39 – When upon life's billows you are tempest tossed…

Hymn 40 – When we walk with the Lord…

Hymn 41 – 'Tis so sweet to trust in Jesus…

Hymn 42 – Jesus keep me in Your love…

Hymn 43 – My faith has found a resting place…

Hymn 44 – What a fellowship, what a joy divine…

Hymn 45 – Sing the wondrous love of Jesus…

Hymn 46 – More about Jesus would I know…

Hymn 47 – Deeper, deeper in the love of Jesus…

Hymn 48 – Are you weary, are you heavyhearted…

Hymn 49 – Through the love of God our Saviour…

Hymn 50 – My hope is built on nothing less…

Hymn 51 – I have found a friend in Jesus…

Hymn 52 – What a friend we have in Jesus…

Hymn 53 – Sweet hour of prayer…

Hymn 54 – All to Jesus I surrender…

Hymn 55 – Take my life and let it be…

Hymn 56 – God moves in a mysterious way…

Hymn 57 – O happy day, that fixed my choice…

Hymn 58 – Amazing grace…

Hymn 59 – Standing on the promises of Christ my King…

Hymn 60 – On a hill far away stood an old rugged cross…

Hymn 61 – We are never, never weary of the grand old song…

01. Hymn of Faithfulness
Tune: Take my life and let it be

1. Faithfulness does not depend
   On what others around do
   It depends on what you do
   Based on what God tells you to

2. Others may do what they do
   You don't have to do the same
   It depends on what you do
   Based on what God tells you to

3. Your reward does not depend
   On how much conformed you are
   It depends on what you do
   Based on what God tells you to

4. God's Kingdom belongs to those
   Who are faithful to the end
   Their tears God will wipe away
   They shall reign forever more

02. Hymn of Answered Prayers
Tune: When I survey the wondrous cross

1. My God answers prayers
   He does answer
   When we ask Him in faith and doubt not
   He turns the tide and speaks to our storms
   The troubled souls, brings He to rest

2. My God answers prayers
   He does answer
   When Hannah in sorrow cried out to Him
   He turned her tide and Samuel was born
   Her troubled soul, He brought to rest

3. My God answers prayers
   He does answer
   When Blind Bartimaeus in anguish cried out
   He turned his tide and granted him sight
   His darkness ended, his light began

4. My God answers prayers
   He still answers
   On Him call in faith He'll answer you too
   He'll turn your tide and speak to your storms
   Your troubled soul, He'll bring to rest.

03. Hymn of Praise

1. I will praise Thee, King of glory
   I will praise Thee, Lord of lords,
   You are faithful, King of glory
   I will praise Thee evermore
2. I will love Thee, King of glory
   I will love Thee, Prince of Peace,
   You are Holy, King of glory
   I will love You evermore
3. I will bless Thee, King of heaven
   I will bless Thee, Lord of Hosts,
   You are mighty, King of heaven
   I will bless Thee evermore
4. I will serve Thee, King of glory
   I will serve Thee, King of kings,
   You are gracious, Precious Master
   I will serve Thee evermore
5. I will trust Thee, Promise-Keeper
   I will trust Thee, El-Shaddai,
   You are faithful, Great Provider
   I will trust You evermore.

04. Hymn of Praise
Tune: There's not a friend like the lowly Jesus

1. Holy Father, so gracious and faithful
   We praise thee 2ce
   Loving Savior, His Blood our sins cleansing
   We praise thee 2ce
   Chorus: Your praise is proclaimed in the Heavens
   Your praise is proclaimed in the earth
   Holy Father, so gracious and faithful
   We praise thee 2ce
2. Great Redeemer, Who rescues and saves us
   We praise thee 2ce
   His love for us is so pure and lofty
   We praise thee 2ce
   Chorus
3. Balm of Gilead, His stripes our wounds healing
   We praise thee 2ce
   Died on the cross our freedom purchasing
   We praise thee 2ce
   Chorus
4. Great Provider, Who supplies all our needs
   We praise thee 2ce
   He cares for us with His great providence

We praise thee 2ce
Chorus

5. Jesus, a Friend Who never forsakes us
We praise thee 2ce
Thy faithfulness, ever sure and steadfast
We praise thee 2ce
Chorus

6. Soon we shall behold Your face in glory
Praising you 2ce
Join with the angels in realms of glory
Praising you 2ce
Chorus

05. Hymn of Worship
Tune: There is none Holy as the Lord

1. Adonai be Thou magnified
For Your love I praise Thee
You're so faithful loving none like Thee
Sovereign Lord, I praise Thy Name

2. El Rapha be Thou lifted high
For Your care I praise Thee
You're so faithful you took my diseases away
My Healer I praise Thy Name

3. El Shalom be Thou exalted
For Your peace I praise Thee
You're so faithful you still the storms of my life
Prince of Peace I praise Thy Name

4. El Jireh be Thou magnified
For Your gifts I praise Thee
You're so faithful all my needs supplying
My Sure Source I praise Thy Name

5. El Sabaoth be Thou lifted high
For Your victory I praise Thee
You're so faithful fighting all my battles
Lord of Hosts I praise Thy Name

06. Hymn of Grace
Tune: There shall be showers of Blessing

1. This is my season of favour
Just as the Lord hath promised
Season of grace for expansion
Breaking new grounds for my Lord

Chorus: Season of favour
Season of favour has come
The One who spoke will never lie
Grace and Mercy, my portion

2. This is my season of mercy
   Just as the Lord hath spoken
   Season of divine compassion
   Sent from the Father of lights
   Chorus

3. This is my season of glory
   Just as the Lord hath spoken
   Shame and reproach, all forgotten
   Hallelujah to my King
   Chorus

4. This is my season of praises
   Angels, join in my glad songs
   Praises for answers to prayers
   Testimonies arriving
   Chorus

07. Hymn of Worship

1. All hail the pow'r of Jesus' name!
   Let angels prostrate fall,
   Let angels prostrate fall;
   Bring forth the royal diadem,
   And crown Him, crown Him,
   crown Him, crown Him;
   And crown Him Lord of all!

2. Ye chosen seed of Israel's race,
   Ye ransomed from the fall,
   Ye ransomed from the fall,
   Hail Him who saves you by His grace,
   And crown Him, crown Him,
   crown Him, crown Him;
   And crown Him Lord of all!

3. Sinners, whose love can ne'er forget
   The wormwood and the gall,
   The wormwood and the gall,
   Go, spread your trophies at His feet,
   And crown Him, crown Him,
   crown Him, crown Him;
   And crown Him Lord of all!

4. Let every kindred, every tribe,
   On this terrestrial ball,
   On this terrestrial ball,
   To Him all majesty ascribe,
   And crown Him, crown Him,
   crown Him, crown Him;
   And crown Him Lord of all!

5. O that with yonder sacred throng
   We at His feet may fall,
   We at His feet may fall!
   We'll join the everlasting song,
   And crown Him, crown Him,
   crown Him, crown Him;

And crown Him Lord of all!

08. Hymn of Praise

1. Praise to the Lord, the Almighty,
the King of creation!
O my soul, praise him, for he is
your health and salvation!
Come, all who hear; now to his
temple draw near,
join me in glad adoration.
2. Praise to the Lord, above all
things so wondrously reigning;
sheltering you under his wings,
and so gently sustaining!
Have you not seen all that is
needful has been
sent by his gracious ordaining?
3. Praise to the Lord, who will
prosper your work and defend
you;
surely his goodness and mercy
shall daily attend you.
Ponder anew what the Almighty
can do,
if with his love he befriends you.
4. Praise to the Lord! O let all that is
in me adore him!
All that has life and breath, come
now with praises before him.
Let the Amen sound from his
people again;
gladly forever adore him.

09. Hymn of Praise

1. Praise, my soul, the King of
heaven;
to his feet your tribute bring.
Ransomed, healed, restored,
forgiven,
evermore his praises sing.
Alleluia, alleluia!
Praise the everlasting King!
2. Praise him for his grace and favor
to his people in distress.
Praise him, still the same as ever,
slow to chide, and swift to bless.
Alleluia, alleluia!
Glorious in his faithfulness!
3. Fatherlike he tends and spares us;
well our feeble frame he knows.
In his hand he gently bears us,
rescues us from all our foes.
Alleluia, alleluia!
Widely yet his mercy flows!
4. Angels, help us to adore him;
you behold him face to face.
Sun and moon, bow down before
him,

dwellers all in time and space.
Alleluia, alleluia!
Praise with us the God of grace!

10. Hymn of Praise

1. O for a thousand tongues to sing
   My great Redeemer's praise,
   The glories of my God and King,
   The triumphs of His grace.
2. My gracious Master and my God,
   Assist me to proclaim,
   To spread through all the earth abroad,
   The honors of Thy name.
3. Jesus! the name that charms our fears,
   That bids our sorrows cease;
   'Tis music in the sinner's ears,
   'Tis life, and health, and peace.
4. His love my heart has captive made,
   His captive would I be,
   For He was bound, and scourged and died,
   My captive soul to free.
5. He breaks the power of canceled sin,
   He sets the prisoner free;
   His blood can make the foulest clean;
   His blood availed for me.
6. So now Thy blessed Name I love,
   Thy will would e'er be mine.
   Had I a thousand hearts to give,
   My Lord, they all were Thine!

11. Hymn of Worship

1. O worship the King all-glorious above,
   O gratefully sing his power and his love:
   our shield and defender, the Ancient of Days,
   pavilioned in splendor and girded with praise.
2. O tell of his might and sing of his grace,
   whose robe is the light, whose canopy space.
   His chariots of wrath the deep thunderclouds form,
   and dark is his path on the wings of the storm.
3. Your bountiful care, what tongue can recite?
   It breathes in the air, it shines in the light;

it streams from the hills, it descends to the plain,
and sweetly distills in the dew and the rain.

4. Frail children of dust, and feeble as frail,
in you do we trust, nor find you to fail.
Your mercies, how tender, how firm to the end,
our Maker, Defender, Redeemer, and Friend!

5. O measureless Might, unchangeable Love,
whom angels delight to worship above!
Your ransomed creation, with glory ablaze,
in true adoration shall sing to your praise!

12. Hymn of Praise

1. Praise Him! praise Him! Jesus, our blessed Redeemer!
Sing, ye saints! His wonderful love proclaim!
Hail Him! hail Him! mightiest angels in glory;
Strength and honor give to His holy name!
Like a shepherd, Jesus will feed His people,
In His arms He carries them all day long;
O ye saints that live in the light of His presence,
Praise Him! praise Him! ever in joyful song!

2. Praise Him! praise Him! Jesus, our blessed Redeemer,
For our sins He suffered and bled and died;
He, our Rock, our Hope of eternal salvation,
Hail Him! hail Him! Jesus, the Crucified;
Loving Savior, meekly enduring sorrow,
Crowned with thorns that cruelly pierced His brow;
Once for us rejected, despised, and forsaken,
Prince of Glory, ever triumphant now.

3. Praise Him! praise Him! Jesus, our blessed Redeemer,
Heavenly portals, loud with

hosannahs ring!
Jesus, Savior, reigneth for ever and ever;
Crown Him! crown Him! Prophet and Priest and King!
Death is vanquished! Tell it with joy, ye faithful,
Where is now thy victory, boasting grave?
Jesus lives! No longer thy portals are cheerless;
Jesus lives, the mighty and strong to save.

13. Hymn of Praise

1. To God be the glory, great things He hath done,
   So loved He the world that He gave us His Son,
   Who yielded His life our redemption to win,
   And opened the life-gate that all may go in.
   Praise the Lord, praise the Lord,
   Let the earth hear His voice;
   Praise the Lord, praise the Lord,
   Let the people rejoice;
   Oh, come to the Father, through Jesus the Son,
   And give Him the glory; great things He hath done.

2. Oh, perfect redemption, the purchase of blood,
   To every believer the promise of God;
   The vilest offender who truly believes,
   That moment from Jesus a pardon receives.
   Praise the Lord, praise the Lord,
   Let the earth hear His voice;
   Praise the Lord, praise the Lord,
   Let the people rejoice;
   Oh, come to the Father, through Jesus the Son,
   And give Him the glory; great things He hath done.

3. Great things He hath taught us, great things He hath done,
   And great our rejoicing through Jesus the Son;
   But purer, and higher, and greater will be
   Our wonder, our transport when Jesus we see.
   Praise the Lord, praise the Lord,
   Let the earth hear His voice;
   Praise the Lord, praise the Lord,

Let the people rejoice;
Oh, come to the Father, through Jesus the Son,
And give Him the glory; great things He hath done.

14. Hymn of Hope

1. O God, our help in ages past,
   Our hope for years to come,
   Our shelter from the stormy blast,
   And our eternal home.
2. Under the shadow of Thy throne
   Thy saints have dwelt secure;
   Sufficient is Thine arm alone,
   And our defence is sure.
3. Before the hills in order stood,
   Or earth received her frame,
   From everlasting Thou art God,
   To endless years the same.
4. A thousand ages in Thy sight
   Are like an evening gone;
   Short as the watch that ends the night
   Before the rising sun.
5. Time, like an ever-rolling stream,
   Bears all its sons away;
   They fly forgotten, as a dream
   Dies at the opening day.
6. O God, our help in ages past,
   Our hope for years to come,
   Be Thou our guard while life shall last,
   And our eternal home.

15. Hymn of Gratitude

1. "Great is Thy faithfulness," O God my Father,
   There is no shadow of turning with Thee;
   Thou changest not, Thy compassions, they fail not
   As Thou hast been Thou forever wilt be.
   "Great is Thy faithfulness!"
   "Great is Thy faithfulness!"
   Morning by morning new mercies I see;
   All I have needed Thy hand hath provided—
   "Great is Thy faithfulness," Lord, unto me!
2. Summer and winter, and springtime and harvest,
   Sun, moon and stars in their courses above,
   Join with all nature in manifold witness

To Thy great faithfulness, mercy
and love.
"Great is Thy faithfulness!"
"Great is Thy faithfulness!"
Morning by morning new mercies
I see;
All I have needed Thy hand hath
provided—
"Great is Thy faithfulness," Lord,
unto me!

3. Pardon for sin and a peace that
endureth,
Thine own dear presence to cheer
and to guide;
Strength for today and bright hope
for tomorrow,
Blessings all mine, with ten
thousand beside!
"Great is Thy faithfulness!"
"Great is Thy faithfulness!"
Morning by morning new mercies
I see;
All I have needed Thy hand hath
provided—
"Great is Thy faithfulness," Lord,
unto me!

16. Hymn of Gladness

1. I am so glad that our Father in
heaven
Tells of His love in the Book He
has given;
Wonderful things in the Bible I
see,
This is the dearest, that Jesus
loves me.
Refrain:
I am so glad that Jesus loves me,
Jesus loves me, Jesus loves me;
I am so glad that Jesus loves me,
Jesus loves even me.

2. Though I forget Him and wander
away,
Still He follows wherever I stray;
Back to His dear loving arms
would I flee,
When I remember that Jesus loves
me. [Refrain]

3. O, if there's only one song I can
sing,
When in His beauty I see the great
King,
This shall my song in eternity be:
O, what a wonder that Jesus loves
me! [Refrain]

17. Hymn of Adoration

1. How sweet the name of Jesus sounds,
   Blessed be the name of the Lord;
   It soothes his sorrows heals his wounds,
   Blessed be the name of the Lord;
   Chorus
   Blessed be the name, blessed be the name,
   Blessed be the name of the Lord;
   Blessed be the name, blessed be the name,
   Blessed be the name of the Lord;

2. It makes the wounded spirit whole,
   Blessed be the name of the Lord;
   'Tis manna to the hungry soul,
   Blessed be the name of the Lord.
   Chorus
   Blessed be the name, Blessed be the name,
   Blessed be the name of the Lord;
   Blessed be the name, Blessed be the name,
   Blessed be the name of the Lord;

3. It soothes the troubled sinner's breast,
   Blessed be the name of the Lord;
   It gives the weary sweetest rest,
   Blessed be the name of the Lord.
   Chorus
   Blessed be the name, Blessed be the name,
   Blessed be the name of the Lord;
   Blessed be the name, Blessed be the name,
   Blessed be the name of the Lord.

4. Then will I tell the sinners round,
   Blessed be the name of the Lord;
   What a dear Saviour I have found,
   Blessed be the name of the Lord.
   Chorus
   Blessed be the name, Blessed be the name,
   Blessed be the name of the Lord;
   Blessed be the name, Blessed be the name,
   Blessed be the name of the Lord.

18. Hymn of Encouragement

1. How sweet the name of Jesus sounds
   in a believer's ear!
   It soothes our sorrows, heals our wounds,
   and drives away our fear.

2. It makes the wounded spirit whole
   and calms the troubled breast;
   'tis manna to the hungry soul,
   and to the weary, rest.
3. O Jesus, shepherd, guardian, friend,
   my Prophet, Priest, and King,
   my Lord, my Life, my Way, my End,
   accept the praise I bring.
4. How weak the effort of my heart,
   how cold my warmest thought;
   but when I see you as you are,
   I'll praise you as I ought.
5. Till then I would your love proclaim
   with every fleeting breath;
   and may the music of your name
   refresh my soul in death.

19. Hymn of Worship

1. Crown Him with many crowns,
   The Lamb upon His throne;
   Hark! how the heav'nly anthem drowns
   All music but its own!
   Awake, my soul, and sing
   Of Him who died for thee,
   And hail Him as thy matchless King
   Through all eternity.
2. Crown Him the Virgin's Son,
   The God Incarnate born,
   Whose arm those crimson trophies won
   Which now His brow adorn:
   Fruit of the mystic Tree,
   As of that Tree the Stem;
   The Root whence flows Thy mercy free,
   The Babe of Bethlehem.
3. Crown Him the Lord of Love:
   Behold His hands and side;
   Rich wounds yet visible above
   In beauty glorified:
   No angel in the sky
   Can fully bear that sight,
   But downward bends his burning eye.
   At mysteries so bright.
5. Crown Him the Lord of peace,
   Whose power a scepter sways
   From pole to pole, that wars may cease,
   And all be prayer and praise.
   His reign shall know no end,
   And round His pierced feet

Fair flowers of glory now extend
Their fragrance ever sweet.

6. Crown Him the Lord of years,
The Potentate of time.
Creator of the rolling spheres,
Ineffably sublime.
All hail, Redeemer, hail!
For Thou hast died for me;
Thy praise shall never, never fail
Throughout eternity.

20. Hymn of Trust

1. There's not a Friend like the lowly Jesus:
   No, not one! no, not one!
   None else could heal all our souls' diseases:
   No, not one! no, not one! Jesus knows all about our struggles;
   He will guide 'til the day is done:
   There's not a Friend like the lowly Jesus:
   No, not one! no, not one!

2. No friend like Him is so high and holy,
   No, not one! no, not one!
   And yet no friend is so meek and lowly,
   No, not one! no, not one! Jesus knows all about our struggles;
   He will guide 'til the day is done:
   There's not a Friend like the lowly Jesus:
   No, not one! no, not one!

3. There's not an hour that He is not near us,
   No, not one! no, not one!
   No night so dark, but His love can cheer us,
   No, not one! no, not one! Jesus knows all about our struggles;
   He will guide 'til the day is done:
   There's not a Friend like the lowly Jesus:
   No, not one! no, not one!

4. Did ever saint find this Friend forsake him?
   No, not one! no, not one!
   Or sinner find that He would not take him?
   No, not one! no, not one! Jesus knows all about our struggles;
   He will guide 'til the day is done:
   There's not a Friend like the lowly Jesus:
   No, not one! no, not one!

5. Was e'er a gift like the Savior given?
   No, not one! no, not one!
   Will He refuse us the bliss of heaven?
   No, not one! no, not one! Jesus knows all about our struggles;
   He will guide 'til the day is done:
   There's not a Friend like the lowly Jesus:
   No, not one! no, not one!

21. Hymn of Impartation

1. Breathe on me, Breath of God,
   Fill me with life anew,
   That I may love what Thou dost love,
   And do what Thou wouldst do.
2. Breathe on me, Breath of God,
   Until my heart is pure,
   Until with Thee I will one will,
   To do and to endure.
3. Breathe on me, Breath of God,
   Till I am wholly Thine,
   Until this earthly part of me
   Glows with Thy fire divine.
4. Breathe on me, Breath of God,
   So shall I never die,
   But live with Thee the perfect life
   Of Thine eternity.

22. Hymn of Provision

1. There shall be showers of blessing:
   This is the promise of love;
   There shall be seasons refreshing,
   Sent from the Savior above.
   Refrain:
   Showers of blessing,
   Showers of blessing we need:
   Mercy-drops round us are falling,
   But for the showers we plead.
2. There shall be showers of blessing,
   Precious reviving again;
   Over the hills and the valleys,
   Sound of abundance of rain.
3. There shall be showers of blessing;
   Send them upon us, O Lord;
   Grant to us now a refreshing,
   Come, and now honor Thy Word.
4. There shall be showers of blessing:
   Oh, that today they might fall,
   Now as to God we're confessing,
   Now as on Jesus we call!

5. There shall be showers of blessing,
   If we but trust and obey;
   There shall be seasons refreshing,
   If we let God have His way.

23. Hymn of Healing

1. The great Physician now is near,
   The sympathizing Jesus;
   He speaks the drooping heart to cheer,
   Oh, hear the voice of Jesus.
   Refrain:
   Sweetest note in seraph song,
   Sweetest name on mortal tongue;
   Sweetest carol ever sung,
   Jesus, blessed Jesus.

2. Your many sins are all forgiv'n,
   Oh, hear the voice of Jesus;
   Go on your way in peace to heav'n,
   And wear a crown with Jesus.

3. All glory to the dying Lamb!
   I now believe in Jesus;
   I love the blessed Savior's name,
   I love the name of Jesus.

4. His name dispels my guilt and fear,
   No other name but Jesus;
   Oh, how my soul delights to hear
   The charming name of Jesus.

5. And when to that bright world above,
   We rise to see our Jesus,
   We'll sing around the throne of love
   His name, the name of Jesus.

24. Hymn of Revival

1. Thy kingdom come, O God,
   thy rule, O Christ, begin;
   break with thine iron rod
   the tyrannies of sin.

2. Where is thy reign of peace
   and purity and love?
   When shall all hatred cease,
   as in the realms above?

3. When comes the promised time
   that war shall be no more,
   and lust, oppression, crime
   shall flee thy face before?

4. We pray thee, Lord, arise,
   and come in thy great might;
   revive our longing eyes,
   which languish for thy sight.

5. Men scorn thy sacred name,
   and wolves devour thy fold;

by many deeds of shame
we learn that love grows cold.
6. O'er lands both near and far
thick darkness broodeth yet:
arise, O Morning Star,
arise, and never set!

25. Hymn of Purification

1. Have you been to Jesus for the cleansing pow'r?
Are you washed in the blood of the Lamb?
Are you fully trusting in His grace this hour?
Are you washed in the blood of the Lamb? Are you washed in the blood,
In the soul-cleansing blood of the Lamb?
Are your garments spotless? Are they white as snow?
Are you washed in the blood of the Lamb?

2. Are you walking daily by the Savior's side?
Are you washed in the blood of the Lamb?
Do you rest each moment in the Crucified?
Are you washed in the blood of the Lamb? Are you washed in the blood,
In the soul-cleansing blood of the Lamb?
Are your garments spotless? Are they white as snow?
Are you washed in the blood of the Lamb?

3. When the Bridegroom cometh will your robes be white!
Are you washed in the blood of the Lamb?
Will your soul be ready for His presence bright,
And be washed in the blood of the Lamb? Are you washed in the blood,
In the soul-cleansing blood of the Lamb?
Are your garments spotless? Are they white as snow?
Are you washed in the blood of the Lamb?

4. Lay aside the garments that are stained with sin,
And be washed in the blood of the Lamb;
There's a fountain flowing for the

soul unclean,
O be washed in the blood of the Lamb. Are you washed in the blood,
In the soul-cleansing blood of the Lamb?
Are your garments spotless? Are they white as snow?
Are you washed in the blood of the Lamb?

26. Hymn of Provision

1. Lord, I hear of show'rs of blessing
   Thou art scatt'ring full and free,
   Show'rs the thirsty land refreshing;
   Let some drops now fall on me.
   Even me, even me,
   Let some drops now fall on me.
2. Pass me not, O gracious Father!
   Sinful though my heart may be;
   Thou might'st leave me, but the rather
   Let Thy mercy fall on me.
   Even me, even me,
   Let some drops now fall on me.
3. Pass me not, O tender Savior!
   Let me love and cling to Thee;
   I am longing for Thy favor;
   While Thou'rt calling, call for me.
   Even me, even me,
   Let some drops now fall on me.
4. Pass me not, O Lord, the Spirit!
   Thou canst make the blind to see;
   By the Witness of Thy merit,
   Speak the word of power to me.
   Even me, even me,
   Let some drops now fall on me.
5. Love of God, so pure and changeless!
   Blood of Christ, so rich and free!
   Grace of God, so strong and boundless!
   Magnify them all in me.
   Even me, even me,
   Let some drops now fall on me.
6. Pass me not! Thy lost one bringing,
   Bind my heart, O Lord, to Thee;
   While the streams of life are springing,
   Blessing others, oh, bless me.
   Even me, even me,
   Let some drops now fall on me.

27. Hymn of Protection

1. Rock of Ages, cleft for me,
   Let me hide myself in Thee;
   Let the water and the blood,
   From Thy riven side which flowed,

    Be of sin the double cure,
    Save me from its guilt and power.

2. Not the labor of my hands
    Can fulfill Thy law's demands;
    Could my zeal no respite know,
    Could my tears forever flow,
    All could never sin erase,
    Thou must save, and save by grace.

3. Nothing in my hands I bring,
    Simply to Thy cross I cling;
    Naked, come to Thee for dress,
    Helpless, look to Thee for grace:
    Foul, I to the fountain fly,
    Wash me, Savior, or I die.

4. While I draw this fleeting breath,
    When mine eyes shall close in death,
    When I soar to worlds unknown,
    See Thee on Thy judgment throne,
    Rock of Ages, cleft for me,
    Let me hide myself in Thee.

28. Hymn of Salvation

1. Jesus only is our message,
    Jesus all our theme shall be;
    We will lift up Jesus ever,
    Jesus only will we see. Jesus only,
    Jesus ever,
    Jesus all in all we sing,
    Savior, Sanctifier, and Healer,
    Glorious Lord and coming King.

2. Jesus only is our Savior,
    All our guilt He bore away,
    He, our righteousness forever,
    All our strength from day to day. Jesus only, Jesus ever,
    Jesus all in all we sing,
    Savior, Sanctifier, and Healer,
    Glorious Lord and coming King.

3. Jesus is our Sanctifier,
    Saving us from self and sin,
    And with all His Spirit's fulness,
    Filling all our hearts within. Jesus only, Jesus ever,
    Jesus all in all we sing,
    Savior, Sanctifier, and Healer,
    Glorious Lord and coming King.

4. Jesus only is our Healer,
    All our sicknesses He bare,
    And His risen life and fulness,
    All His members still may share. Jesus only, Jesus ever,
    Jesus all in all we sing,
    Savior, Sanctifier, and Healer,
    Glorious Lord and coming King.

5. Jesus only is our Power,
    He the gift of Pentecost;
    Jesus, breathe Thy pow'r upon us,

Fill us with the Holy Ghost. Jesus only, Jesus ever,
Jesus all in all we sing,
Savior, Sanctifier, and Healer,
Glorious Lord and coming King.

6. And for Jesus we are waiting,
List'ning for the Advent Call;
But 'twill still be Jesus only,
Jesus ever, all in all. Jesus only, Jesus ever,
Jesus all in all we sing,
Savior, Sanctifier, and Healer,
Glorious Lord and coming King.

29. Hymn of Deliverance

1. Would you be free from your burden of sin?
There's power in the blood, power in the blood;
Would you o'er evil a victory win?
There's wonderful power in the blood.
There is power, power, wonder-working power,
In the blood of the Lamb;
There is power, power, wonder-working power,
In the precious blood of the Lamb.

2. Would you be free from your passion and pride?
There's power in the blood, power in the blood;
Come for a cleansing to Calvary's tide,
There's wonderful power in the blood.
There is power, power, wonder-working power,
In the blood of the Lamb;
There is power, power, wonder-working power,
In the precious blood of the Lamb.

3. Would you be whiter, much whiter than snow?
There's power in the blood, power in the blood;
Sin-stains are lost in its life-giving flow,
There's wonderful power in the blood.
There is power, power, wonder-working power,
In the blood of the Lamb;
There is power, power, wonder-working power,
In the precious blood of the Lamb.

4. Would you do service for Jesus your King?
There's power in the blood, power in the blood;
Would you live daily His praises to sing?
There's wonderful power in the blood.
There is power, power, wonder-working power,
In the blood of the Lamb;
There is power, power, wonder-working power,
In the precious blood of the Lamb.

30. Hymn of Salvation

1. We have heard the joyful sound:
Jesus saves! Jesus saves!
Spread the tidings all around:
Jesus saves! Jesus saves!
Bear the news to every land,
Climb the steeps and cross the waves;
Onward! – 'tis our Lord's command;
Jesus saves! Jesus saves!

2. Waft it on the rolling tide,
Jesus saves, Jesus saves;
Tell to sinners far and wide,
Jesus saves, Jesus saves;
Sing, ye islands of the sea,
Echo back, ye ocean caves;
Earth shall keep her jubilee,
Jesus saves, Jesus saves.

3. Sing above the battle's strife,
Jesus saves, Jesus saves;
By His death and endless life,
Jesus saves, Jesus saves;
Sing it softly thru the gloom,
When the heart for mercy craves,
Sing in triumph o'er the tomb,
Jesus saves, Jesus saves.

4. Give the winds a mighty voice,
Jesus saves, Jesus saves;
Let the nations now rejoice.
Jesus saves, Jesus saves;
Shout salvation full and free,
Highest hills and deepest caves,
This our song of victory,
Jesus saves, Jesus saves.

31. Hymn of Prayer

1. I'm pressing on the upward way,
New heights I'm gaining ev'ry day;
Still praying as I'm onward bound,
"Lord, plant my feet on higher ground."

Refrain:

Lord, lift me up, and let me stand
By faith, on heaven's tableland;
A higher plane than I have found,
Lord, plant my feet on higher ground.

2. My heart has no desire to stay
Where doubts arise and fears dismay;
Though some may dwell where these abound,
My prayer, my aim, is higher ground. [Refrain]

3. I want to live above the world,
Though Satan's darts at me are hurled;
For faith has caught a joyful sound,
The song of saints on higher ground.
[Refrain]

4. I want to scale the utmost height,
And catch a gleam of glory bright;
But still I'll pray till heav'n I've found,
"Lord, lead me on to higher ground."
[Refrain]

Hymn 32. Hymn of Assurance

1. Blessed assurance, Jesus is mine!
Oh, what a foretaste of glory divine!
Heir of salvation, purchase of God,
born of his Spirit, washed in his blood.

Refrain:

This is my story, this is my song,
praising my Savior all the day long.
This is my story, this is my song,
praising my Savior all the day long.

2. Perfect communion, perfect delight,
visions of rapture now burst on my sight.
Angels descending bring from above
echoes of mercy, whispers of love. [Refrain]

3. Perfect submission, all is at rest.
I in my Savior am happy and bless'd,
watching and waiting, looking above,
filled with his goodness, lost in his love. [Refrain]

33. Hymn of Prayer

1. I need Thee ev'ry hour,
   Most gracious Lord;
   No tender voice like Thine
   Can peace afford.
   Refrain:
   I need Thee, oh, I need Thee;
   Ev'ry hour I need Thee;
   Oh, bless me now, my Savior,
   I come to Thee.

2. I need Thee ev'ry hour,
   Stay Thou nearby;
   Temptations lose their pow'r
   When Thou art nigh. [Refrain]

3. I need Thee ev'ry hour,
   In joy or pain;
   Come quickly and abide,
   Or life is vain. [Refrain]

4. I need Thee ev'ry hour,
   Teach me Thy will;
   And Thy rich promises
   In me fulfill. [Refrain]

34. Hymn of Comfort

1. When peace like a river attendeth my way,
   when sorrows like sea billows roll;
   whatever my lot, thou hast taught me to say,
   "It is well, it is well with my soul."
   Refrain (may be sung after final stanza only):
   It is well with my soul;
   it is well, it is well with my soul.

2. Though Satan should buffet,
   though trials should come,
   let this blest assurance control:
   that Christ has regarded my helpless estate,
   and has shed his own blood for my soul. Refrain

3. My sin oh, the bliss of this glorious thought!
   my sin, not in part, but the whole,
   is nailed to the cross, and I bear it no more;
   praise the Lord, praise the Lord, O my soul! Refrain

4. O Lord, haste the day when my faith shall be sight,
   the clouds be rolled back as a scroll;
   the trump shall resound and the Lord shall descend;
   even so, it is well with my soul. Refrain

35. Hymn of Warfare

1. Onward, Christian soldiers,
   marching as to war,
   With the cross of Jesus
   going on before!
   Christ, the royal Master,
   leads against the foe;
   Forward into battle,
   see his banner go!
   Refrain:
   Onward, Christian soldiers,
   marching as to war,
   With the cross of Jesus
   going on before!

2. At the sign of triumph
   Satan's host doth flee;
   On, then, Christian soldiers,
   on to victory!
   Hell's foundations quiver
   at the shout of praise;
   Brothers, lift your voices,
   loud your anthems raise! [Refrain]

3. Like a mighty army
   moves the church of God;
   Brothers, we are treading
   where the saints have trod;
   We are not divided;
   all one body we,
   One in hope and doctrine,
   one in charity. [Refrain]

4. Onward, then, ye people,
   join our happy throng,
   Blend with ours your voices
   in the triumph song;
   Glory, laud, and honor,
   unto Christ the King;
   This thro' countless ages
   men and angels sing. [Refrain]

36. Hymn of Warfare

1. Stand up, stand up for Jesus! ye
   soldiers of the cross;
   Lift high His royal banner, it must
   not suffer loss:
   From vict'ry unto vict'ry, His army
   shall He lead,
   Till every foe is vanquished, and
   Christ is Lord indeed.

2. Stand up, stand up for Jesus! The
   trumpet call obey:
   Forth to the mighty conflict, in this
   His glorious day;
   Ye that are men now serve Him
   against unnumbered foes;
   Let courage rise with danger, and
   strength to strength oppose.

3. Stand up, stand up for Jesus! Stand in His strength alone,
The arm of flesh will fail you, ye dare not trust your own;
Put on the gospel armor, and watching unto prayer,
Where calls the voice of duty, be never wanting there.

4. Stand up, stand up for Jesus! the strife will not be long;
This day the noise of battle, the next the victor's song;
To him that overcometh a crown of life shall be;
He with the King of glory shall reign eternally.

37. Hymn of Prayer

1. Christian, seek not yet repose,
Hear thy gracious Savior say;
Thou art in the midst of foes:
Watch and pray.

2. Principalities and powers,
Mustering their unseen array,
Wait for thy unguarded hours:
Watch and pray.

3. Gird thy heavenly armor on,
Wear it ever night and day;
Ambushed lies the evil one:
Watch and pray.

4. Hear the victors who o'ercame,
Still they mark each warrior's way;
All with one sweet voice exclaim,
Watch and pray.

5. Hear, above all, hear thy Lord,
Him thou lovest to obey;
Hide within thy heart His word:
Watch and pray.

6. Watch, as if on that alone
Hung the issue of the day;
Pray, that help may be sent down:
Watch and pray.

38. Hymn of Love

1. My Jesus, I love Thee, I know Thou art mine;
For Thee all the follies of sin I resign;
My gracious Redeemer, my Savior art Thou;
If ever I loved Thee, my Jesus, 'tis now.

2. I love Thee because Thou hast first loved me,
And purchased my pardon on Calvary's tree;
I love Thee for wearing the thorns on Thy brow;

If ever I loved Thee, my Jesus, 'tis now.

3. I'll love Thee in life, I will love Thee in death,
And praise Thee as long as Thou lendest me breath;
And say when the death dew lies cold on my brow,
If ever I loved Thee, my Jesus, 'tis now.

4. In mansions of glory and endless delight,
I'll ever adore Thee in heaven so bright;
I'll sing with the glittering crown on my brow,
If ever I loved Thee, my Jesus, 'tis now.

39. Hymn of Gratitude

1. When upon life's billows you are tempest tossed,
When you are discouraged, thinking all is lost,
Count your many blessings name them one by one,
And it will surprise you what the Lord hath done.

Count your blessings, name them one by one;
Count your blessings, see what God hath done;
Count your blessings, name them one by one,
And it will surprise you what the Lord hath done.

2. Are you ever burdened with a load of care?
Does the cross seem heavy you are called to bear?
Count your many blessings, every doubt will fly,
And you will be singing as the days go by.

Count your blessings, name them one by one;
Count your blessings, see what God hath done;
Count your blessings, name them one by one,
And it will surprise you what the Lord hath done.

3. When you look at others with their lands and gold,
Think that Christ has promised you His wealth untold.
Count your many blessings, money

cannot buy
Your reward in heaven, nor your Lord on high.
Count your blessings, name them one by one;
Count your blessings, see what God hath done;
Count your blessings, name them one by one,
And it will surprise you what the Lord hath done.

4. So amid the conflict, whether great or small,
Do not be discouraged, God is over all;
Count your many blessings, angels will attend,
Help and comfort give you to your journey's end.
Count your blessings, name them one by one;
Count your blessings, see what God hath done;
Count your blessings, name them one by one,
And it will surprise you what the Lord hath done.

40. Hymn of Trust

1. When we walk with the Lord
In the light of His Word,
What a glory He sheds on our way;
While we do His good will,
He abides with us still,
And with all who will trust and obey. Trust and obey,
For there's no other way
To be happy in Jesus,
But to trust and obey.

2. Not a shadow can rise,
Not a cloud in the skies,
But His smile quickly drives it away;
Not a doubt or a fear,
Not a sigh or a tear,
Can abide while we trust and obey. Trust and obey,
For there's no other way
To be happy in Jesus,
But to trust and obey.

3. Not a burden we bear,
Not a sorrow we share,
But our toil He doth richly repay;
Not a grief or a loss,
Not a frown or a cross,
But is blest if we trust and obey. Trust and obey,

For there's no other way
To be happy in Jesus,
But to trust and obey.

4. But we never can prove
The delights of His love,
Until all on the altar we lay;
For the favor He shows,
And the joy He bestows,
Are for them who will trust and obey. Trust and obey,
For there's no other way
To be happy in Jesus,
But to trust and obey.

5. Then in fellowship sweet
We will sit at His feet,
Or we'll walk by His side in the way;
What He says we will do;
Where He sends, we will go,
Never fear, only trust and obey.
Trust and obey,
For there's no other way
To be happy in Jesus,
But to trust and obey.

41. Hymn of Trust

1. 'Tis so sweet to trust in Jesus,
Just to take Him at His Word;
Just to rest upon His promise,
And to know, "Thus saith the Lord!"
Refrain:
Jesus, Jesus, how I trust Him!
How I've proved Him o'er and o'er;
Jesus, Jesus, precious Jesus!
Oh, for grace to trust Him more!

2. Oh, how sweet to trust in Jesus,
Just to trust His cleansing blood;
And in simple faith to plunge me
'Neath the healing, cleansing flood!
[Refrain]

3. Yes, 'tis sweet to trust in Jesus,
Just from sin and self to cease;
Just from Jesus simply taking
Life and rest, and joy and peace.
[Refrain]

4. I'm so glad I learned to trust Thee,
Precious Jesus, Savior, Friend;
And I know that Thou art with me,
Wilt be with me to the end.
[Refrain]

42. Hymn of Prayer

1. Jesus keep me in Your love
There to dwell forever.
Fill me with Your own Spirit.
There to serve You ever.

Chorus:

In Your love, in Your love

There to dwell forever

Jesus keep me in Your love,

There to dwell forever.

2. Jesus keep me in Your love

A living sacrifice,

Holy, willing, obedient,

There to serve You ever. [Chorus]

3. Jesus keep me in Your love,

Loving You more than life,

Faithful to Thee to the end,

There to serve You ever. [Chorus]

4. Jesus keep me in Your love

Hungering for You only

Thirsting for Your righteousness

There to serve You ever. Amen!

43. Hymn of Faith

1. My faith has found a resting place,

Not in device or creed;

I trust the ever-living One,

His wounds for me shall plead.

Refrain:

I need no other argument,

I need no other plea,

It is enough that Jesus died,

And that He died for me.

2. Enough for me that Jesus saves,

This ends my fear and doubt;

A sinful soul I came to Him,

He'll never cast me out. [Refrain]

3. My heart is leaning on the Word,

The living Word of God,

Salvation by my Savior's name,

Salvation through His blood. [Refrain]

4. My great physician heals the sick,

The lost He came to save;

For me His precious blood He shed,

For me His life He gave. [Refrain]

44. Hymn of Rest

1. What a fellowship, what a joy divine,

Leaning on the everlasting arms;

What a blessedness, what a peace is mine,

Leaning on the everlasting arms.

Refrain:

Leaning, leaning,

Safe and secure from all alarms;

Leaning, leaning,

Leaning on the everlasting arms.

2. Oh, how sweet to walk in this pilgrim way,

Leaning on the everlasting arms;
   Oh, how bright the path grows
   from day to day,
   Leaning on the everlasting arms.
   [Refrain]
3. What have I to dread, what have I
   to fear,
   Leaning on the everlasting arms?
   I have blessed peace with my Lord
   so near,
   Leaning on the everlasting arms.
   [Refrain]

45. Hymn of Hope

1. Sing the wondrous love of Jesus,
   Sing His mercy and His grace;
   In the mansions bright and blessed
   He'll prepare for us a place.
   Refrain:
   When we all get to heaven,
   what a day of rejoicing that will be!
   When we all see Jesus,
   we'll sing and shout the victory!
2. While we walk the pilgrim pathway
   Clouds will overspread the sky;
   But when trav'ling days are over
   Not a shadow, not a sigh. [Refrain]
3. Let us then be true and faithful,
   Trusting, serving ev'ry day;
   Just one glimpse of Him in glory
   Will the toils of life repay.
   [Refrain]
4. Onward to the prize before us!
   Soon His beauty we'll behold;
   Soon the pearly gates will open–
   We shall tread the streets of gold.
   [Refrain]

46. Hymn of Prayer

1. More about Jesus would I know,
   More of His grace to others show;
   More of His saving fullness see,
   More of His love who died for me.
   Refrain:
   More, more about Jesus,
   More, more about Jesus;
   More of His saving fullness see,
   More of His love who died for me.
2. More about Jesus let me learn,
   More of His holy will discern;
   Spirit of God, my teacher be,
   Showing the things of Christ to me.
   [Refrain]
3. More about Jesus, in His Word,
   Holding communion with my Lord;
   Hearing His voice in every line,
   Making each faithful saying mine.
   [Refrain]

4. More about Jesus on His throne,
   Riches in glory all His own;
   More of His kingdom's sure increase;
   More of His coming, Prince of Peace. [Refrain]

47. Hymn of Prayer

1. Deeper, deeper in the love of Jesus
   Daily let me go;
   Higher, higher in the school of wisdom,
   More of grace to know.
   Refrain:
   Oh, deeper yet, I pray,
   And higher every day,
   And wiser, blessed Lord,
   In Thy precious, holy Word.
2. Deeper, deeper, blessed Holy Spirit,
   Take me deeper still,
   Till my life is wholly lost in Jesus,
   And His perfect will. [Refrain]
3. Deeper, deeper! though it cost hard trials,
   Deeper let me go!
   Rooted in the holy love of Jesus,
   Let me fruitful grow. [Refrain]
4. Deeper, higher, every day in Jesus,
   Till all conflict past,
   Finds me conqu'ror, and in His own image
   Perfected at last. [Refrain]
5. Deeper, deeper in the faith of Jesus,
   Holy faith and true;
   In His pow'r and soul exulting wisdom
   Let me peace pursue. [Refrain]

48. Hymn of Prayer

1. Are you weary, are you heavyhearted?
   Tell it to Jesus,
   Tell it to Jesus;
   Are you grieving over joys departed?
   Tell it to Jesus alone.
   Chorus:
   Tell it to Jesus, tell it to Jesus,
   He is a friend that's well known;
   You've no other such a friend or brother,
   Tell it to Jesus alone.
2. Do the tears flow down your cheeks unbidden?
   Tell it to Jesus,
   Tell it to Jesus;
   Have you sins that to men's eyes

are hidden?
Tell it to Jesus alone.
[Chorus]

3. Do you fear the gath'ring clouds of sorrow?
Tell it to Jesus,
Tell it to Jesus;
Are you anxious what shall be tomorrow?
Tell it to Jesus alone.
[Chorus]

4. Are you troubled at the thought of dying?
Tell it to Jesus,
Tell it to Jesus;
For Christ's coming kingdom are you sighing?
Tell it to Jesus alone.
[Chorus]

49. Hymn of Assurance

1. Through the love of God our Saviour,
all will be well.
Free and changeless is his favour,
all, all is well.
Precious is the blood that healed us,
perfect is the grace that sealed us,
strong the hand stretched forth to shield us,
all must be well.

2. Though we pass through tribulation,
all will be well.
Ours is such a full salvation,
all, all is well.
Happy, still in God confiding,
fruitful, if in Christ abiding,
holy, through the Spirit's guiding,
all must be well.

3. We expect a bright tomorrow,
all will be well.
Faith can sing through days of sorrow,
'All, all is well.'
On our Father's love relying,
Jesus every need supplying,
in our living, in our dying,
all must be well.

50. Hymn of Hope

1. My hope is built on nothing less
than Jesus' blood and righteousness;
I dare not trust the sweetest frame,
but wholly lean on Jesus' name.
Refrain:
On Christ, the solid Rock, I stand:

all other ground is sinking sand;
all other ground is sinking sand.

2. When darkness veils his lovely face,
I rest on his unchanging grace;
in every high and stormy gale,
my anchor holds within the veil.
[Refrain]

3. His oath, his covenant, his blood,
support me in the whelming flood;
when all around my soul gives way,
he then is all my hope and stay.
[Refrain]

4. When he shall come with trumpet sound,
O may I then in him be found:
dressed in his righteousness alone,
faultless to stand before the throne.
[Refrain]

51. Hymn of Love

1. I have found a friend in Jesus-
He's ev'rything to me,
He's the fairest of ten thousand to my soul;
The Lily of the Valley- in Him alone I see
All I need to cleanse and make me fully whole.
In sorrow He's my comfort, in trouble He's my stay,
He tells me ev'ry care on Him to roll;
He's the Lily of the Valley, the Bright and Morning Star,
He's the greatest of ten thousand to my soul.

2. He all my grief has taken and all my sorrows borne,
In temptation He's my strong and mighty tow'r;
I have all for Him forsaken and all my idols torn
From my heart, and now He keeps me by His pow'r.
Though all the world forsake me and Satan tempt me sore,
Through Jesus I shall safely reach the goal;
He's the Lily of the Valley, the Bright and Morning Star,
He's the greatest of ten thousand to my soul.

3. He will never, never leave me nor yet forsake me here,
While I live by faith and do His blessed will;
A wall of fire about me, I've

nothing now to fear-
With His manna He my hungry soul shall fill.
Then sweeping up to glory I'll see His blessed face,
Where rivers of delight shall ever roll;
He's the Lily of the Valley, the Bright and Morning Star,
He's the greatest of ten thousand to my soul.

52. Hymn of Prayer

1. What a friend we have in Jesus,
   All our sins and griefs to bear!
   What a privilege to carry
   Everything to God in prayer!
   Oh, what peace we often forfeit,
   Oh, what needless pain we bear,
   All because we do not carry
   Everything to God in prayer!

2. Have we trials and temptations?
   Is there trouble anywhere?
   We should never be discouraged—
   Take it to the Lord in prayer.
   Can we find a friend so faithful,
   Who will all our sorrows share?
   Jesus knows our every weakness;
   Take it to the Lord in prayer.

3. Are we weak and heavy-laden,
   Cumbered with a load of care?
   Precious Savior, still our refuge—
   Take it to the Lord in prayer.
   Do thy friends despise, forsake thee?
   Take it to the Lord in prayer!
   In His arms He'll take and shield thee,
   Thou wilt find a solace there.

4. Blessed Savior, Thou hast promised
   Thou wilt all our burdens bear;
   May we ever, Lord, be bringing
   All to Thee in earnest prayer.
   Soon in glory bright, unclouded,
   There will be no need for prayer—
   Rapture, praise, and endless worship
   Will be our sweet portion there.

53. Hymn of Prayers

1. Sweet hour of prayer! sweet hour of prayer!
   That calls me from a world of care,
   And bids me at my Father's throne
   Make all my wants and wishes known.
   In seasons of distress and grief,

My soul has often found relief,
And oft escaped the tempter's snare,
By thy return, sweet hour of prayer!

2. Sweet hour of prayer! sweet hour of prayer!
The joys I feel, the bliss I share,
Of those whose anxious spirits burn
With strong desires for thy return!
With such I hasten to the place
Where God my Savior shows His face,
And gladly take my station there,
And wait for thee, sweet hour of prayer!

3. Sweet hour of prayer! sweet hour of prayer!
Thy wings shall my petition bear
To Him whose truth and faithfulness
Engage the waiting soul to bless.
And since He bids me seek His face,
Believe His Word and trust His grace,
I'll cast on Him my every care,
And wait for thee, sweet hour of prayer!

4. Sweet hour of prayer! sweet hour of prayer!
May I thy consolation share,
Till, from Mount Pisgah's lofty height,
I view my home and take my flight.
This robe of flesh I'll drop, and rise
To seize the everlasting prize,
And shout, while passing through the air,
"Farewell, farewell, sweet hour of prayer!"

54. Hymn of Surrender

1. All to Jesus I surrender,
All to Him I freely give;
I will ever love and trust Him,
In His presence daily live.
Refrain:
I surrender all, I surrender all;
All to Thee, my blessed Savior,
I surrender all.

2. All to Jesus I surrender,
Make me, Savior, wholly Thine;
Let me feel Thy Holy Spirit,
Truly know that Thou art mine.
[Refrain]

3. All to Jesus I surrender,
Lord, I give myself to Thee;

Fill me with Thy love and power,
Let Thy blessing fall on me.
[Refrain]

55. Hymn of Dedication

1. Take my life and let it be
   consecrated, Lord, to thee.
   Take my moments and my days;
   let them flow in endless praise,
   let them flow in endless praise.
2. Take my hands and let them move
   at the impulse of thy love.
   Take my feet and let them be
   swift and beautiful for thee,
   swift and beautiful for thee.
3. Take my voice and let me sing
   always, only, for my King.
   Take my lips and let them be
   filled with messages from thee,
   filled with messages from thee.
4. Take my silver and my gold;
   not a mite would I withhold.
   Take my intellect and use
   every power as thou shalt choose,
   every power as thou shalt choose.
5. Take my will and make it thine;
   it shall be no longer mine.
   Take my heart it is thine own;
   it shall be thy royal throne,
   it shall be thy royal throne.
6. Take my love; my Lord, I pour
   at thy feet its treasure store.
   Take myself, and I will be
   ever, only, all for thee,
   ever, only, all for thee.

56. Hymn of Providence

1. God moves in a mysterious way
   His wonders to perform;
   He plants His footsteps in the sea
   And rides upon the storm.
2. Deep in unfathomable mines
   Of never failing skill
   He treasures up His bright designs
   And works His sov'reign will.
3. Ye fearful saints, fresh courage take;
   The clouds ye so much dread
   Are big with mercy and shall break
   In blessings on your head.
4. Judge not the Lord by feeble sense,
   But trust Him for His grace;
   Behind a frowning providence
   He hides a smiling face.
5. His purposes will ripen fast,
   Unfolding every hour;

The bud may have a bitter taste,
But sweet will be the flow'r.

6. Blind unbelief is sure to err
And scan His work in vain;
God is His own interpreter,
And He will make it plain.

57. Hymn of Joy

1. O happy day, that fixed my choice
On Thee, my Savior and my God!
Well may this glowing heart rejoice,
And tell its raptures all abroad.
Refrain:
Happy day, happy day,
When Jesus washed my sins away!
He taught me how to watch and pray,
And live rejoicing every day:
Happy day, happy day,
When Jesus washed my sins away!

2. O happy bond, that seals my vows
To Him Who merits all my love!
Let cheerful anthems fill His house,
While to that sacred shrine I move.
[Refrain]

3. 'Tis done, the great transaction's done!—
I am the Lord's and He is mine;
He drew me and I followed on;
Charmed to confess the voice divine. [Refrain]

4. Now rest, my long-divided heart,
Fixed on this blissful center, rest;
Here have I found a nobler part;
Here heav'nly pleasures fill my breast. [Refrain]

5. High heav'n, that heard the solemn vow,
That vow renewed shall daily hear,
Till in life's latest hour I bow
And bless in death a bond so dear.

58. Hymn of Grace

1. Amazing grace (how sweet the sound)
that saved a wretch like me!
I once was lost, but now am found,
was blind, but now I see.

2. 'Twas grace that taught my heart to fear,
and grace my fears relieved;
how precious did that grace appear
the hour I first believed!

3. Through many dangers, toils and snares
I have already come:
'tis grace has brought me safe thus

far,
and grace will lead me home.

4. The Lord has promised good to me,
his word my hope secures;
he will my shield and portion be
as long as life endures.

5. Yes, when this flesh and heart shall fail,
and mortal life shall cease:
I shall possess, within the veil,
a life of joy and peace.

6. The earth shall soon dissolve like snow,
the sun forbear to shine;
but God, who called me here below,
will be forever mine.

59. Hymn of Faith

1. Standing on the promises of Christ my King,
Through eternal ages let His praises ring,
Glory in the highest, I will shout and sing,
Standing on the promises of God.
Refrain:
Standing, standing,
Standing on the promises of God my Savior;
Standing, standing,
I'm standing on the promises of God.

2. Standing on the promises that cannot fail,
When the howling storms of doubt and fear assail,
By the living Word of God I shall prevail,
Standing on the promises of God.
[Refrain]

3. Standing on the promises I now can see
Perfect, present cleansing in the blood for me;
Standing in the liberty where Christ makes free,
Standing on the promises of God.

4. Standing on the promises of Christ the Lord,
Bound to Him eternally by love's strong cord,
Overcoming daily with the Spirit's sword,
Standing on the promises of God.

5. Standing on the promises I cannot fall,
List'ning every moment to the

Spirit's call,
Resting in my Savior as my all in all,
Standing on the promises of God.

60. Hymn of Dedication

1. On a hill far away stood an old rugged cross,
the emblem of suffering and shame;
and I love that old cross where the dearest and best
for a world of lost sinners was slain.
Refrain:
So I'll cherish the old rugged cross,
till my trophies at last I lay down;
I will cling to the old rugged cross,
and exchange it some day for a crown.

2. O that old rugged cross, so despised by the world,
has a wondrous attraction for me;
for the dear Lamb of God left his glory above
to bear it to dark Calvary. [Refrain]

3. In that old rugged cross, stained with blood so divine,
a wondrous beauty I see,
for 'twas on that old cross Jesus suffered and died,
to pardon and sanctify me.
[Refrain]

4. To that old rugged cross I will ever be true,
its shame and reproach gladly bear;
then he'll call me some day to my home far away,
where his glory forever I'll share.
[Refrain]

61. Hymn of Praise

1. We are never, never weary of the grand old song;
Glory to God, hallelujah!
We can sing it loud as ever, with our faith more strong;
Glory to God, hallelujah!
Refrain
O, the children of the Lord have a right to shout and sing,
For the way is growing bright, and our souls are on the wing;
We are going by and by to the palace of a King!
Glory to God, hallelujah!

2. We are lost amid the rapture of redeeming love
Glory to God, hallelujah!

We are rising on its pinions to the hills above:

Glory to God, hallelujah! [Refrain]

3. We are going to a palace that is built of gold;

 Glory to God, hallelujah!

 Where the King in all His splendor we shall soon behold

 Glory to God, hallelujah! [Refrain]

4. There we'll shout redeeming mercy in a glad, new song;

 Glory to God, hallelujah!

 There we'll sing the praise of Jesus with the blood washed throng;

 Glory to God, hallelujah! [Refrain]

SAY THIS ALOUD:

"My Father, You alone deserve all my worship and praises. I will sing unto You all the days of my life.

Accept my songs in Jesus' Name."

50 Promises of God Available to all Believers

1. **Isaiah 55:5**

   "Surely you shall call a nation you do not know, and nations who do not know you shall run to you, because of the LORD your God, and the Holy One of Israel; for He has glorified you."

2. **Isaiah 58:11**

   "The LORD will guide you continually, and satisfy your soul in drought, and strengthen your bones; you shall be like a watered garden, and like a spring of water, whose waters do not fail."

3. **Isaiah 54:4**

   "Do not fear, for you will not be ashamed, nor be disgraced, for you will not be put to shame; for you will forget the shame of your youth; and will not remember the reproach of your widowhood anymore".

4. **Isaiah 54: 13-14**

   "All your children shall be taught by the LORD, and great shall be the peace of you children. In righteousness you shall be established; you shall be far from oppression, for you shall not fear, and from terror, for it shall not come near you."

5. **Isaiah 54:17a**

   "No weapon formed against you shall prosper, and every tongue which rises against you in judgment you shall condemn."

6. **Isaiah 43:2**

   "When you pass through the waters, I will be with you; and through the rivers, they shall not overflow you. When you walk through the fire, you shall not be burned, nor shall the flame scorch you."

7. **Isaiah 43:18-19**

   "Do not remember the former things, nor consider the things of old. Behold, I will do a new thing; now it shall spring forth; shall you not know it? I will even make a road in the wilderness and rivers in the desert."

8. **Job 8:7**

   "Though your beginning was small, yet your latter end would increase abundantly."

9. **Job 8:22a**

   "Those who hate you will be clothed with shame…"

10. **Psalm 32:8**

    "I will instruct you and teach you in the way you should go; I will guide you with My eye."

11. **Isaiah 30:21**

    "Your ears shall hear a word behind you, saying, 'This is the way, walk in it', whenever you turn to the right hand or whenever you turn to the left."

12. **Isaiah 49:15-16**

    "Can a woman forget her nursing child, and not have compassion on the son of her womb? Surely they may forget, yet I will not forget you. See, I have inscribed you on the palms of My hands; your walls are continually before Me."

13. Isaiah 49:24-26

"Shall the prey be taken from the mighty, or the captives of the righteous be delivered? But thus says the LORD; 'Even the captives of the mighty shall be taken away, and the prey of the terrible be delivered; for I will contend with him who contends with you, and I will save your children. I will feed those who oppress you with their own flesh, and they shall be drunk with their own blood as with sweet wine. All flesh shall know that I, the LORD, am your Savior and your Redeemer, the Mighty One of Jacob."

14. Isaiah 66:9

"'Shall I bring to the time of birth, and not cause delivery?' says the LORD. 'Shall I who cause delivery shut up the womb?' says your God."

15. Jeremiah 1:8

"Do not be afraid of their faces, for I am with you to deliver you; says the LORD."

16. Joshua 1:3a

"Every place that the sole of your foot will tread upon I have given you..."

17. Joshua 1:9

"Have I not commanded you? Be strong and of good courage; do not be afraid, nor be dismayed, for the LORD your God is with you wherever you go."

18. **Jeremiah 1:19**

"They will fight against you, but they shall not prevail against you. For I am with you, says the LORD, to deliver you."

19. **Jeremiah 29:11-12**

"For I know the thoughts that I think toward you, says the LORD, 'thoughts of peace and not of evil, to give you a future and a hope.' Then, you will call upon Me and go and pray to Me, and I will listen to you."

20. **Jeremiah 31:17a**

"'There is hope in your future,' says the LORD."

21. **Jeremiah 33:3**

"Call to Me, and I will answer you, and show you great and mighty things, which you do not know."

22. **Ezekiel 12:25,28**

"For I am the LORD, I speak, and the word which I speak will come to pass; it will no more be postponed; for in your days…I will say the word and perform it; says the Lord God."

"…Thus says the Lord God, 'None of My words will be postponed any more, but the word which I speak will be done', says the Lord God."

23. **Ezekiel 18:21**

"But if a wicked man turns from all his sins which he has committed, keeps all My statutes, and does what is lawful and right, he shall surely live; he shall not die."

24. Joel 2:26

"You shall eat in plenty and be satisfied, and praise the name of the LORD your God, who has dealt wondrously with you; and My people shall never be put to shame."

25. Nahum 1:9

"What do you conspire against the LORD? He will make an utter end of it. Affliction will not rise up a second time."

26. Zephaniah 3:19

"Behold, at that time, I will deal with all who afflict you; I will save the lame, and gather those who were driven out; I will appoint them for praise and fame in every land where they were put to shame."

27. Zechariah 1:3

"…Thus says the LORD of hosts; Return to Me, says the LORD of hosts, and I will return to you, says the LORD of hosts."

28. Malachi 3:6

"For I am the LORD, I do not change; therefore you are not consumed, O sons of Jacob."

29. Malachi 4:2

"But to you who fear My name the Sun of Righteousness shall arise with healing in His wings; and you shall go out and grow fat like stall – fed calves."

30. Isaiah 3:10

"Say to the righteous that it shall be well with them, for they shall eat the fruit of their doings."

31. 2 Chronicles 7:14

"If My people who are called by My name will humble themselves, and pray and seek My face and turn from their wicked ways, then I will hear from heaven, and will forgive their sin and heal their land."

32. Genesis 12:2-3

"I will make you a great nation; I will bless you and make your name great; and you shall be a blessing. I will bless those who bless you, and I will curse him who curses you; and in you all the families of the earth shall be blessed."

33. Matthew 18:18-19

"Assuredly, I say to you, whatever you bind on earth will be bound in heaven, and whatever you loose on earth will be loosed in heaven. Again, I say to you that if two of you agree on earth concerning anything that they shall ask, it will be done for them by My Father in heaven."

34. Matthew 19:29

"And everyone who has left houses or brothers or sisters or father or mother or wife or children or lands for My name's sake shall receive a hundredfold, and inherit everlasting life."

35. Matthew 21:22

"And all things, whatever you ask in prayer, believing, you will receive."

36. Matthew 24:35

"Heaven and earth will pass away, but My words will by no means pass away."

37. Matthew 28:20b

"I am with you always, even to the end of the age."

38. Luke 11:13

"If you then, being evil, know how to give good gifts to your children, how much more will your heavenly Father give the Holy Spirit to those who ask Him!"

39. John 6:37

"All that the Father gives Me will come to Me, and the one who comes to Me I will by no means cast out."

40. John 7:38

"He who believes in Me, as the Scripture has said, out of his heart will flow rivers of living water."

41. John 12:26

"If anyone serves Me, let him follow Me; and where I am, there My servant will be also. If anyone serves Me, him My Father will honor."

42. John 14:26

"But the Helper, the Holy Spirit, whom the Father will send in My name, He will teach you all things, and bring to your remembrance all things that I said to you."

43. John 15:17

"If you abide in Me, and My words abide in you, you will ask what you desire; and it shall be done for you."

44. John 16:33

"These things I have spoken to you, that in Me you may have peace. In the world you will have tribulation; but be of good cheer, I have overcome the world."

45. Matthew 7:7

"Ask, and it will be given to you; seek, and you will find; knock, and it will be opened to you."

46. James 1:5

"If any of you lacks wisdom, let him ask of God, who gives to all liberally and without reproach, and it will be given to him."

47. Revelation 3:20

"Behold, I stand at the door and knock. If anyone hears My voice and opens the door, I will come in to him and dine with him and he with Me."

48. Isaiah 40:29

"He gives power to the weak, and to those who have no might He increases strength."

49. Isaiah 41:10,13

"Fear not, for I am with you; be not dismayed, for I am your God; I will strengthen you, yes I will help you, I will uphold you with My righteous right hand. For I, the LORD your God, will hold your right hand, saying to you, 'Fear not, I will help you.'"

50. Revelation 22:12

"And behold, I am coming quickly, and My reward is with Me, to give everyone according to his work."

Conclusion

These promises are meant to be claimed because they are actually ours as God's children. As regards their fulfillment, Numbers 23:19 has taken care of that. It says 'God is not a man that He should lie; neither the son of man that He should repent; hath He said, and shall He not do it? or hath He spoken, and shall He not make good?' Also, Proverbs 30:5 GNT says 'God keeps every promise He makes…'
So, we can be sure that He will do what He has promised.

However, these promises may not be fulfilled in a person's life if such a person starts dishonoring or disregarding the One who made the promises. A very good example is in 1 Samuel 2:30; "Therefore the LORD God of Israel says: 'I said indeed that your house and the house of your father would walk before Me forever;' but now the LORD says: Far be it from Me; for those who honor Me I will honor, and those who despise Me shall be lightly esteemed."

You see, it is a very terrible thing to have God withdraw His good promises from an individual. Eli did not respect God and he lost those beautiful promises.

In this dispensation, the greatest honor you can give to God is to gladly accept His precious and sacrificial Gift to humanity – His only begotten Son, Jesus Christ. Accepting Jesus Christ into your life is the greatest of all the honor you can give to God; and with Jesus, all of God's promises are surely going to be fulfilled in your life.

Romans 8:32 AMP says 'He who did not spare [even] His own Son, but gave Him up for us all, how will He not also, along with Him, graciously give us all things?'

And 2 Corinthians 1:20 ERV says 'The yes to all of God's promises is in Christ. And that is why we say "Amen" through Christ to the glory of God.'

So, if you are willing to do that now, you can quickly say this prayer:

<u>*"Lord Jesus, I am a sinner. Please have mercy on me and cleanse me by Your precious Blood of atonement. Kindly erase my name from the book of death and write it in the Book of Life. I accept You as my personal Lord and Saviour; and by Your grace, I promise to live the rest of my life bringing You glory. Thank You for saving me."*</u>

Yes, you are now qualified to enjoy the fulfillment of all the good promises God has made concerning you in His Word. Start claiming them now; they will be fulfilled in your life and you will praise the Lord. Hallelujah!

BECOME A FINANCIAL PARTNER WITH JESUS

At *Global Emancipation Ministries - Calgary*, our mandate is *to liberate men through the knowledge of the Truth* and our mission statement is *creating channels through which men can encounter the Truth - Isaiah 61:1-3; John 8:32, 36; I Thessalonians 5:24.*

Our Ministerial Activities include engagement in Evangelical Outreaches, Church Meetings, Teaching of the undiluted Word of God, Discipleship, Social Media Witnessing, Podcasting, Publishing of Gospel Materials, Jesus Shows, Internet Ministry, Believers' Conferences, Worship Sessions, Spiritual Life Coaching among other Christian ministry programs - all geared towards getting people to know and experience the only One ordained by God the Father to redeem and grant absolute freedom to mankind - Jesus Christ.

If you sense the Lord is calling you to reach out to the lost by engaging in any of these activities or by assisting those involved with your resources, please feel free to join us. Let us come together as we take the Gospel of our Lord Jesus Christ to the hurting and forgotten ones.
[Mark 16:15-20].

Please join us in these kingdom projects by making your weekly, monthly, quarterly or annual donations to:
Global Emancipation Ministries – Calgary
TD Canada Trust (TD Bank)
5247676
You can also visit the "GIVE" section on our website, www.gloem.org**, to learn about other ways to give.**

For acknowledgement, please advise your donations or cheques to us by email: info@gloem.org, and kindly include your details i.e. name, address, email and location. Alternatively, you can simply call +1 587 9735910 to do same.

You can also volunteer your gifts and talents in the service of the Lord through our ministerial platforms regardless of your location. To get information on how to go about this, please visit www.gloem.org or send us an email via info@gloem.org. God bless you.

ABOUT THE AUTHOR

By the special grace of God, **Anthony O. Adefarakan** is the privileged President of **Global Emancipation Ministries - Calgary (GLOEM)** with headquarters in Canada, North America and **Emancipating Truth Ministry International (ETMI)** with headquarters in Nigeria, West Africa.

The Lord called him into the field ministry in February 2008 with the mandate to liberate men through the knowledge of the Truth, and by December 2012 he was ordained and commissioned as the Pioneer Pastor – in – Charge of The Redeemed Christian Church of God, Revelation Parish, Shalom Area under Delta Province III, Nigeria where he served until 1st February 2015 when he officially handed over to a new Pastor in order to focus on his field ministry to which the Lord had earlier called him and for which the authority of the church had already prayed and released him to undertake.

On 29th September 2013, he was awarded a Post Graduate Diploma in Tent – Making Mission from the Redeemed Christian School of Missions, Nigeria (RECSOM, Asaba Campus) where he also had the privilege to train Pastors and Missionaries as a lecturer in 2017.

Since the commissioning of his field ministry in 2015 he has had the opportunity to lead his ministry officers to field ministrations in different Prisons, Hospitals,

Orphanages, Rural communities, Camp settlements, Markets, Local churches among other places with great successes on all occasions – such as salvation of sinners, healing of the sick, financial empowerment of mission churches, provision of relief materials to the poor, provision of medical services to the underprivileged, baptism in the Holy Ghost, deliverance from demonic oppression, release of inmates just to mention a few - all to the glory of God Who alone is the Doer.

He is the author of other best-selling titles such as *The Law of Kinds, It's Your Size, The Immutability of God's Counsel, Surely there is an End, Life Applicable lessons from the Book of Ruth, One thing is Needful, Life Applicable Revelations from God's Word* among others.

He is happily married to Ifeoluwa A. Adefarakan and their marriage is fruitful to the glory of God.

Jesus is his Message, Freedom is the Outcome!

Isaiah 61:1-3.

www.gloem.org

Scan the QR Codes below to access other Life Transforming Publications

NOTES

NOTES

NOTES

NOTES

NOTES

NOTES

NOTES

NOTES

NOTES

NOTES

NOTES

NOTES

NOTES

NOTES

www.ingramcontent.com/pod-product-compliance
Lightning Source LLC
Chambersburg PA
CBHW070341010526
44107CB00004B/588